PRAISE FOR THE DIAGRAMS BOOK

"If you process things visually as I do, or if you deal with people who do, you need to communicate your ideas in a simple and effective way. This book will help you do your job better."

Chris Carmichael, Media Director, EMEA at Hewlett-Packard

"Geometry turned into an engaging strategic toolkit. This is a fun and richly rewarding read."

Richard Swaab, Executive Vice Chairman AMVBBDO

"I love it - It's great - really innovative. I dip in and out during the day and work out how I can use this stuff in presentations."

Simon Redfern, Director of Corporate Affairs, Starbucks

"Kevin is a crystal clear thinker who specializes in simplifying the complex. Here he turns his attention to the visual language of business, showing the reader how to crack problems and communicate with precision. Highly recommended."

David Simoes-Brown & Roland Harwood, Founders, 100% Open

"I had been coveting a copy for a while, so I am dead chuffed to actually get my hands on one."

Richard Huntington, Director of Planning, Saatchi & Saatchi

"I'm a big fan of visuals to help represent a point, so it really did the job."

Mat Sears, Head of PR and Corporate Communications, Everything Everywhere

To Rosanna, Shaunagh and Sarah, my RSS feed.

THE
DIAGRAMS
BOOK

50 ways to solve
any problem visually

Kevin Duncan

LONDON   **NEW YORK**   **SHANGHAI**
MADRID   **BARCELONA**   **BOGOTA**
MEXICO CITY   **MONTERREY**   **BUENOS AIRES**

Published by
LID Publishing Ltd.
The Loft, 19a Floral Street
Covent Garden
London WC2E 9DS
United Kingdom
info@lidpublishing.com
www.lidpublishing.com

A member of:

BPR
Business Publishers Roundtable

www.businesspublishersroundtable.com

© Kevin Duncan 2013, 2014
© LID Publishing Ltd. 2013, 2014

Reprinted 2013, 2014

Printed in the Czech Republic by Finidr

ISBN: 978-1-907794-29-2

Cover design: e-Digital Design Ltd
Page design: e-Digital Design Ltd

CONTENTS

Part Four: TIMELINES & YEAR VIEWS

Part Five: FLOWS & CONCEPTS

FOREWORD

· · · · · · · · · · · · · · ·

I am delighted Kevin has written this book. I love shapes as a way of expressing thoughts or ideas – it's the way my brain works. I think visually. Diagrams help to keep my thinking clear and simple, and I'm a big believer in keeping things simple.

With standing still no longer an option, we're all under pressure to get more done. Yet the world is more complicated and getting things done is more of a challenge. I regularly talk to clients about the "how" being more of a challenge than the "what".

If we want to get more things done we need to simplify, and there lies the value of a good diagram – a simple visual representation of a strategy, thought or idea. We should embrace wholeheartedly any tools that help us to get things done, so this book is for anyone who wants to get stuff done.

People only remember 10% of what they read, but 30% of what they see. Shapes have an immediate advantage over words. And yet most businesses tend to focus on the written word. Don't get me wrong – I like words as much as the next person, but words can be, and often are, abused. There can be a temptation to write too much and that can make things complicated. Diagrams can be abused too, but not to the same degree. I believe thinking visually helps get to the simplicity of a thought.

I'm delighted Kevin has included all my favourite diagrams – circles, the classic pyramid, the funnel and the bow tie.

I started off my early marketing career using circles (great for target audiences), and the pie chart continues to be an easy way to understand sales breakdowns quickly. Concentric circles will always be useful, as the world doesn't always fit into neat and separate entities.

The pyramid immediately makes me think of Maslow's Hierarchy of Needs. I've used that many times to explain thoughts and ideas. As part of a team a few years ago, we used Maslow's Hierarchy to win a pitch for a big paint manufacturer – we explained how women saw colour and home design as a way of self-expression.

The bow tie is a good one. In its simplest form it represents lots of inputs, condensed into one simple expression or idea, then expressed back out into many different forms. It's really useful for marketers who need to use different data sources to develop an idea, and then activate that in many different ways.

Shapes and diagrams travel, and in a world where globalization is affecting many of us, that's important. Those of us in global businesses need our thinking to be able to work across borders, and there lies the value of visuals.

We are becoming a more visual society. More and more of us will be thinking visually in the years to come. We will all be embracing shapes and diagrams as a way of thinking.

If I were to leave you with one last shape that represents my thoughts on this book it would be ♥.

Tracy De Groose, CEO, Carat UK

INTRODUCTION

· · · · · · · · · · · · · · · · · · · ·

Having trained thousands of people, it is apparent that many find it hard to express ideas and solve problems purely with words.

They find it easier to use diagrams. It's a form of visual thinking.

This is a compendium of the most popular and useful designs, compiled over thirty years.

I hope you find them useful. Keep me posted on how you get on, and if you enjoy this book, do look at *The Ideas Book* too.

thediagramsbook.com

PART ONE

TRIANGLES AND PYRAMIDS

A WORD ON
TRIANGLES
AND PYRAMIDS

The triangle is a design classic.

It captures the essence of any 1, 2, 3 or A, B, C sequence so beloved of people the world over.

Three blind mice. An Englishman, an Irishman and a Scotsman walk into a bar. *The Lord of the Rings* trilogy. Everybody loves things that come in threes.

So if any three-pronged issue requires explanation, try a triangle.

But there's more.

Wedges can dramatize gradual increases or declines – building a story up, or narrowing options down.

Interlocking two triangles can show a mixture of both, or a transition from one state of affairs to another.

Pyramids can explain gradation and the components of a progression.

And, rather brilliantly, the space in the middle of a triangle offers a chance for a fourth component – most powerfully, the focal point of the issue in question.

1 **THE PYRAMID**

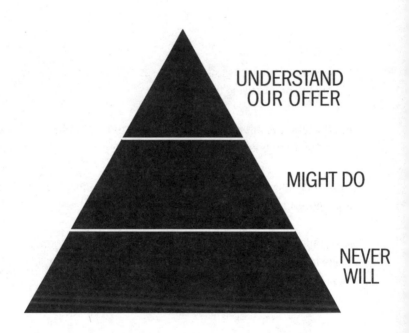

UNDERSTAND OUR OFFER

MIGHT DO

NEVER WILL

- The pyramid is one of the most versatile diagrams in the world.
- The base offers a platform, the middle a transition area, and the peak, (or capstone), an achievement, a destination, or an elite group.

- It is very useful for categorizing discrete groups without overcomplicating matters.
- In this example, the top section represents people who understand a company's offer, the middle is people who might, and the base is people who never will. By populating the sections with prospect names or quantities, the viewer has an immediate grasp of what the new business strategy should be.
- Classically, high volume or mass market subjects will be at the base, with effort concentrating the higher one goes.
- The top usually represents a target or aspiration of some kind.
- The most rigorous versions are diligent enough to populate each layer with numbers, so that the size of the opportunity, or lack of it, is absolutely clear.

Exercise: Choose an issue. Divide it into no fewer than three, and no more than five, stages, categories or segments. Put them in sequence. Choose a direction from top to bottom of the pyramid or vice versa. Add quantities to each layer if relevant.

2 THE SELLING PYRAMID

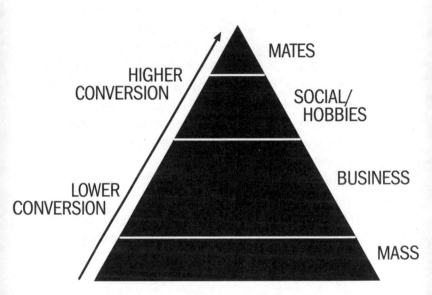

- Pyramids can be given multiple layers. For clarity, it is best not to have more than five layers, otherwise the information will become too cluttered.
- The selling pyramid is a good way to work out where to deploy your sales efforts.

- In this simple example, the size of the segment radiates downward from knowing a few close friends at the top, and then expanding in size via social and business contacts to arrive at a mass audience.
- Quantifying these sections helps someone who runs their own business to work out what to concentrate on, but is equally useful for large businesses.
- Direction and nature of opportunity can be added by including an arrow. In this case, the point being made is that the likelihood of converting to a sale will increase the more closely connected the potential purchaser is to the business owner.

Exercise: Choose a product, brand or service you wish to sell. Use The Selling Pyramid to define who might buy it. Put them in sequence from a small to a large opportunity. Add quantities if possible for each layer, and then choose your easiest or most profitable segment as the place to start.

3 THE CONE OF LEARNING

- The Cone of Learning was conceived by Edgar Dale in 1969.
- It uses the scale of the pyramid to make a number of points about how well (or poorly) we retain knowledge, in this case two weeks after being taught.
- The tiny tip of the pyramid is used to show that after this time we only remember 10% of what we read.
- This increases to 20% of what we hear, 30% of what we see, 50% of what we see *and* hear, and 70% of what we say.
- The large wide base is used to make the clinching point – that after two weeks we retain 90% of what we say *and* do.
- The space in the sections is used to give examples of what the nature of the learning techniques might be in each case.
- The system can be used for working out the right medium to use depending on the importance of the point you want to make, progressing from small at the top to large at the base.
- The moral is you can always increase your communication effectiveness by stepping up the medium you use. If you want your point to really stick then don't hide behind email. If you were going to send an email, then call. If you were going to call, then meet. If you can't meet, use modern technology to replicate those conditions, with a video call or webinar.

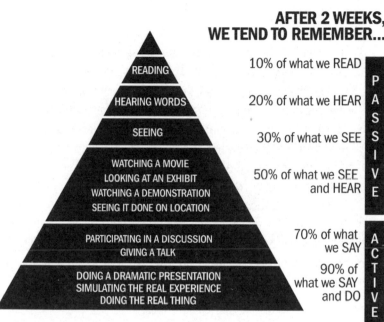

**AFTER 2 WEEKS,
WE TEND TO REMEMBER...**

READING

HEARING WORDS

SEEING

WATCHING A MOVIE
LOOKING AT AN EXHIBIT
WATCHING A DEMONSTRATION
SEEING IT DONE ON LOCATION

PARTICIPATING IN A DISCUSSION
GIVING A TALK

DOING A DRAMATIC PRESENTATION
SIMULATING THE REAL EXPERIENCE
DOING THE REAL THING

10% of what we READ

20% of what we HEAR

30% of what we SEE

50% of what we SEE
and HEAR

70% of what
we SAY

90% of
what we SAY
and DO

P A S S I V E

A C T I V E

Exercise: Choose a point you really need to get across effectively. Use The Cone of Learning to set yourself a minimum target of 50% memory of your message after two weeks (see and hear), and work out the best way to achieve this. For a more ambitious version, set yourself a 90% target (say and do) to yield the optimum result.

4 THE WHITTLING WEDGE

- The Whittling Wedge is brilliant for telling a strategic story and narrowing down options. This allows the presenter to explain their workings, show that a lot was considered, but still end with a clear, preferably single, recommendation.
- Starting on the left, many options can be introduced, analyzed, and then systematically rejected, using as much rationale and detail as is appropriate to the subject.
- By the middle of the wedge, we should be down to a maximum of three or four possibilities.
- These can be analyzed in even more detail, or even recommended for detailed research.
- Finally the presenter arrives on the right with a beautifully argued recommendation that has covered all considerations.

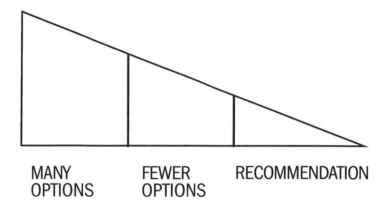

MANY
OPTIONS

FEWER
OPTIONS

RECOMMENDATION

Exercise: Choose a presentation or story that needs explaining, ideally one with quite a few options or wide-ranging subject matter. Use The Whittling Wedge to start broad, and then reduce the number of options or topics systematically. Try to arrive at the end with one clear recommendation or point of view.

5 THE RISING WEDGE

- The Rising Wedge is ideal for building a story, or demonstrating how something will develop over time.
- The steepness of the incline can be varied to indicate speed over a shorter time span.
- It can also be used as a partner to The Whittling Wedge, by expanding a story outward. For example, having whittled to the essence of a recommendation, the presenter can then explain how the idea can be used in many different formats, with multiple audiences, in different regions, and so on.
- As with a pyramid, the recommended maximum number of subdivisions is five, in order to retain clarity.
- In this example, we examine the classic adoption sequence of a new product or craze. Early adopters are the first to get going, followed by the secondary and late adopters, followed at the end by the laggards.
- These sections are at their most powerful when populated by figures.

- Here we see that the majority of the market opportunity comes later, so a brand would be well advised to be patient.
- Data like these enable the presenter to tell a compelling strategic story, or explain where future effort should be expended in a convincing way.

Exercise: Choose a time period or point that needs expanding. Divide The Rising Wedge by time or segments. Add figures if relevant. Practice expanding the story from left to right.

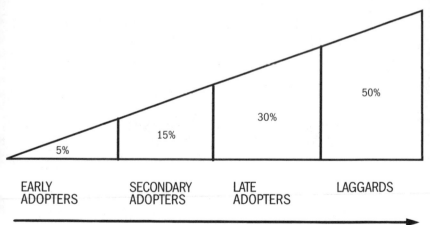

6 THE INTERLOCKING WEDGE

- The Interlocking Wedge allows two diametrically opposed approaches to be compared logically.
- The two extremes are placed to the far right and left, approaches A and B. At each extreme the approach taken would be 100% A or B.
- A manageable number of interlocking criteria are then chosen, in this case three: high (100% one approach), medium (60% one, 40% the other) and low (80:20).

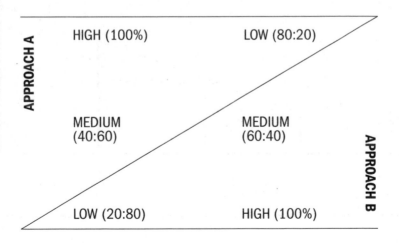

- By merging these criteria from left to right and vice versa, the diagram generates a series of possible permutations for resolving the issue.
- In this example there are six permutations, and each can then be analyzed for suitability.

Exercise: *Choose an issue with two extremes. Place one at each end of The Interlocking Wedge. Choose a maximum of three permutations that deal with different ways in which the problem can be approached. Give the permutations a percentage ratio and place them above or below the diagonal as appropriate depending on severity. Review the different combinations and choose which will work best.*

7 THE IF TRIANGLE

- The IF Triangle is a crucial ally in any negotiation because it covers the only three variables that are ever at stake when a customer is considering whether to make a purchase.

- The three questions are always:
  Will it do the job? (quality)
  How much will it cost? (price)
  When can I have it? (timing)

- When negotiating, there can always be some flexibility on any two of these variables, but never on all three.
- For example, the price can usually be reduced if more time is allowed. Quicker delivery may be possible for a premium price. And although no one will ever admit to wanting low quality, things can often be short-circuited.
- It is called the IF Triangle because a good way to enact a successful negotiating stance is to start every sentence in the negotiation with the word *If*.
- It is impossible to finish a sentence that begins with *If* without attaching a condition – a crucial weapon in any successful negotiation.
- Examples include: *"If I have to deliver it by Friday, the price will have to increase"*, and *"If you need the price to reduce, I will need longer to do the job"*.

Exercise: *Choose an issue that is the subject of negotiation. Write down the time, cost and quality parameters. Devise three sentences beginning with "If..." that define your negotiation stance.*

8 THE F TRIANGLE

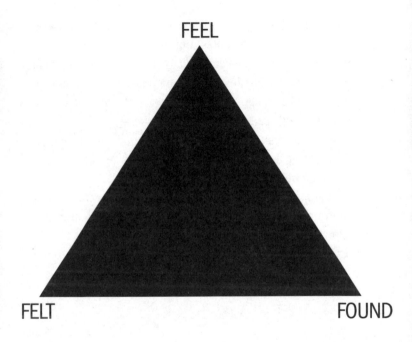

FEEL

FELT

FOUND

- The F Triangle is extremely helpful for overcoming objections to a sale.
- The three components are feel, felt, and found.
- The idea is to compose a sentence that encourages a sceptical customer to reconsider their reservations and end up buying after all.

- The construction of the sentence will run along these lines: "I understand you *feel* x about subject y – I *felt* the same but once I discovered z I *found* it was more than worth the money."
- The personal 'I' can be replaced with the views of colleagues or other influencers, and the discovery element can be expressed as an experience, a product feature, or an emotional benefit.

Exercise: Choose a situation in which the potential customer doesn't want to buy from you or your company, or one in which they have significant doubts. Articulate how you feel about the subject, how others felt the same, and identify what they found to overcome their reservations and lead to a sale. Now compose the sentence.

9 THE BUSINESS
SATISFACTION TRIANGLE

- The Business Satisfaction Triangle deals with the three most important components that affect whether companies and their people find their work fulfilling.
- The three elements are fun (enjoyment), subject matter (intellectual interest and stimulation), and financial value (making a profit).
- If a business can tick all three criteria, then it has ideal work circumstances.
- It is important that a minimum of two of these criteria are met to make any project or customer relationship appealing.
- If only one can be ticked, then the business should seriously consider declining the work, or at the very least must change something significant.
- If none of the criteria apply, then the business should probably not proceed.

FINANCIAL VALUE

SUBJECT MATTER · FUN

Exercise: Choose a client relationship, or a potential one. Use the three criteria to tick, score or predict their outcome. See how many criteria apply. Now decide whether to proceed with the relationship, or make important changes.

10 THE PERSONAL MOTIVATION TRIANGLE

RECOGNITION

JOB SATISFACTION   FINANCIAL REWARD

- The Personal Motivation Triangle is ideal for use in appraisals when assessing morale and staff motivation in a member of staff or a team.
- It can also be used to assess your own personal circumstances.

- It maps out the three most important components that affect whether people find their work fulfilling.
- The three elements are recognition (status, progression and promotion), job satisfaction (intellectual interest and stimulation), and financial reward (salary and benefits).
- If an individual can tick all three, then they have the ideal work circumstances.
- If they are happy with two of these criteria then attention can be paid to improving the third.
- If only one can be ticked, then urgent and significant change is needed.
- If none apply, then either the employer should be acting urgently, or the individual should probably move job immediately if nothing can be changed.

Exercise: *If you are conducting an appraisal, ask the person you are appraising to conduct the exercise, and examine the results to find out what matters to them most. Use the findings as a basis for discussion or action. Design a graded scoring system if necessary. If you are doing it for yourself, take the three criteria and decide how happy you are with each of them. See how acute the problem is and then work out what needs to be changed.*

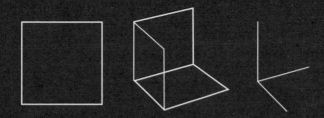

PART TWO

SQUARES AND AXES

A WORD ON
SQUARES
AND AXES
·····················

There's nothing square about squares.

One straight line can express time or direction.

Two can provide horizontal and vertical axes.

Make them cross and you have a grid.

Add more and you have a square.

Grids generate quadrants and are great for separating elements and mapping markets.

Two axes with different attributes can be overlaid, and the exercise can be repeated many times until clarity is revealed.

Culture plays a part in which quadrant is viewed as the most desirable – top right is favoured in most of the Western world, whereas Arabic countries read right to left.

Scale can be adjusted to dramatize the size of the problem or opportunity.

11 THE GROWING PANE

GOOD

CONFIRM RELEVANCE AND KEEP	REAFFIRM RELEVANCE AND USE TO INSPIRE MORE
GET RID OF IMMEDIATELY	ANALYZE WHY, LEARN LESSONS AND DESIGN NEW ONES

OLD   NEW

BAD

- This diagram helps to disentangle the good and bad elements of your working life, the business practices of a company, or even your personal habits.
- The vertical axis represents good at the top, and bad at the bottom.
- The horizontal axis represents old on the left, and new on the right.
- The pane allows you to categorize processes, techniques, or habits. If something is old and good, then it goes in the top left quadrant, and so on.

- If you have several practices in the 'good and old' segment, then that is fine. They have obviously stood the test of time, and do the job.
- If you have several of them in the 'good and new' section, even better. This means you are generating new ideas that really work. A blend of old and new is healthy.
- If there is anything in the 'new and bad' area, it needs careful analysis. It takes guts to reject an idea or process that has only recently been introduced, but surgery here is almost certainly necessary.
- Anything in the 'old and bad' quadrant is clearly not working and should be dropped immediately.

Exercise: *Choose a subject to analyze. Select a manageable number of items to review – no more than 10 or 12. Work through them allocating each one to the relevant quadrant. Write an action list based on what needs to be done as a result.*

12 THE PRIORITY MATRIX

URGENT

DELEGATE
OR DO FIRST, QUICKLY

DO NOW

NOT
IMPORTANT

IMPORTANT

IGNORE OR CANCEL

THINK AND PLAN

NOT URGENT

- The Priority Matrix helps establish what order of priority you are going to give to the jobs on your checklist.
- It can equally be applied to a day, a week, a month, or even a year.
- The vertical axis represents urgent/not urgent, and the horizontal one is important/not important.
- If it is urgent and important, it falls in the top right, and you should do it now. The precise definition of 'now' may vary. Start with today and put the tasks in priority order.

- If it is urgent but not important, delegate it if you can, or do it quickly first to get it out of the way and meet the deadline.
- If it is important but not urgent, think about what you need to do and plan when you are going to do it. Be sure to put this planned time into your diary immediately – do not delay it and thus create yet another task.
- If it is neither important nor urgent, then you should question why you are doing it at all. If possible, ignore or cancel these tasks.

Exercise: *Take your list of things to do. Choose a helpful time period, such as a day, week or month. Draw the diagram and place each task in the appropriate quadrant. Methodically work through the action, starting with the most urgent.*

13 THE MARKET MAP

- The Market Map is a highly effective and very flexible way to establish clarity and strategic authority when looking at any market.
- Start by selecting two important factors in the market in question. For example, in the automotive market these might be price and safety reputation.
- Plot two overlapping axes from high to low, always placing the high ends to the top and right.
- Place your company and any competitors on the grid. So in this example a car with a good safety reputation and a high price would appear top right.
- Use the results to identify gaps in the market, or significant overlaps. Being out on your own could either be good (more distinctive) or bad (what do the others know that you don't?)
- If presenting to win a pitch, pointing out some current deficiencies and explaining how your proposals will improve matters (moving towards the top right) can be very powerful.

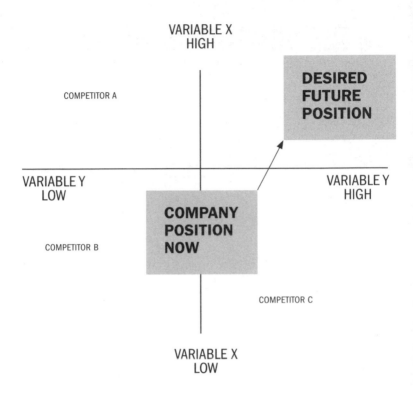

VARIABLE X
HIGH

COMPETITOR A

**DESIRED
FUTURE
POSITION**

VARIABLE Y
LOW

VARIABLE Y
HIGH

**COMPANY
POSITION
NOW**

COMPETITOR B

COMPETITOR C

VARIABLE X
LOW

***Exercise:** Choose a market or category to look at. Choose your first two variables. Place your company or brand, and your competitors, on the grid. Repeat as often as desired with different variables and new combinations. Examine the results, decide where the best opportunities are and what the next appropriate action is.*

14 THE BARGAINING ARENA

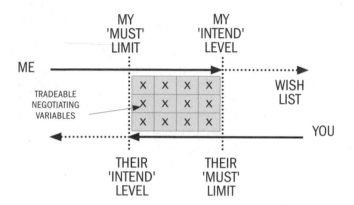

- The Bargaining Arena is excellent for preparing for a negotiation.
- View yourself or your company as being on the left of the diagram, with the other person or company approaching the issue from the right.
- The first point on the negotiation line is your 'must' limit – the limit below which you simply cannot go. So, for example, if it is a financial negotiation and you are selling on a product or service that you have bought in for £7,000, then £7,000 is your bare minimum.
- The next point is your 'intend' level – the amount you intend to get. In this example this might be £9,000 to allow a sensible margin on the transaction.

- Your wish list area includes any other benefits you would wish to have if the negotiation is going particularly well.
- Plotting the other negotiator's likely 'must', 'intend' and wish list points creates an overlap area in the centre.
- This is The Bargaining Arena, where a series of tradeable negotiating variables can be identified and used to bargain with. Trading these will allow both parties to come away satisfied.

Exercise: *Choose a negotiation topic. Work out your minimum 'must' limit. Now add your 'intend' level. Think of a wish list to add if you succeed in achieving your 'must' and 'intend' early. Repeat the exercise imagining you are the other party. Look at the overlapping needs and conclude what you believe the most important negotiating variables to be. Now plan your negotiating approach.*

15 THE BRAVERY SCALE

```
0 |_____|_____|_____| 10
  CONSERVATIVE          AVERAGE              BRAVE
```

- The Bravery Scale is a good way to establish how adventurous projects or proposals should be before a lot of time and effort is spent preparing them.
- The project leader or proposal writer asks three questions:
  1. How adventurous is the company culture?
  2. What standards are expected?
  3. How brave should the targets be?
- A score out of ten is generated to see whether conservative (below 5), average (5-7), or brave (above 7) levels are desired.
- The scores can be blended to create one overall figure. For example, a conservative company asking for brave work may need to have its scale weighted downward to reflect their overall conservatism.
- The three questions can of course be varied to suit the nature of the work.

- When the work is reaching conclusion, the scale helps to remind all present what level of bravery was requested in the first place, and provides a measure with which to compare.
- The scale is particularly useful to both sides in a service relationship such as a client and agency, where the bravery of work is frequently under discussion.

Exercise: Choose a client or a proposal. Consider what questions would provide the most helpful guide. Ask the person or team who will be receiving the proposal to answer them. Use the responses to inform colleagues who are working on the proposal what is expected. Judge the ideas against the scale before deciding which to present and use the scale to frame expectations when presenting.

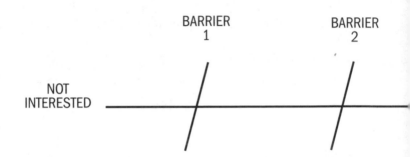

- Lines and axes can be helpful to demonstrate a progression from one state of affairs to another.
- In the Barriers To Purchase Axis, inactivity or disinterest is shown on the left, and interest or action on the right.
- Each notch of the axis represents a barrier to action. In this case it's a series of reasons why the potential customer will not purchase a product.
- By mapping the decision-making process diagrammatically, each barrier to purchase can be identified and isolated.
- A plan to knock each one down can then be devised.

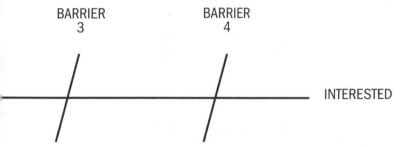

BARRIER
3

BARRIER
4

INTERESTED

Exercise: Choose a product and a potential customer type. Use the axis to plot all the reasons stopping someone from purchasing. If relevant, put the barriers to purchase in chronological order, or place the biggest or hardest ones first, to the far left. Then come up with a plan to knock down each barrier.

17 THE BOX PROCESS

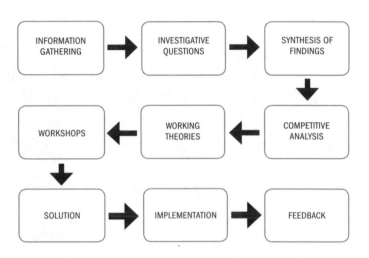

- The Box Process enables any work system to be explained simply.
- Each box contains a stage of work to be done. The descriptions inside them should be short and clear, and durations can be added to each if helpful.
- Each stage is linked by a directional arrow that shows what happens next, and it is important that the sequence is accurate.
- In this example there are nine stages, moving from information gathering through working theories to implementation and feedback.

- A cost per stage can be added to each box to help clarify the value of each.
- A process needs to have a minimum of three stages to make the chart worthwhile; one with over nine stages is likely to be too complex.

Exercise: Take a process and break it down into stages. Place each stage in a box, make sure the sequence is correct, and link them with arrows. Make the descriptions as simple as possible. Add durations and costs per stage if helpful. Test-drive on a colleague to make sure all is clear.

18 THE LONG TAIL

- The Long Tail was described by Chris Anderson in the book of the same name in 2006.
- The received wisdom in most markets is that high volume 'hits' are the best way to make money, as in a million-selling album.
- Anderson's Long Tail theory pointed out that the arrival of the internet had removed the need for much of the infrastructure required to generate and support a hit, such as costly premises, storage facilities, distribution, packaging, labour, and so on.
- Instead, a 'long tail' of many niche products selling at modest volumes can actually add up to more sales in total than the one-off hit.
- Overall, use of The Long Tail diagram helps to identify the pros and cons of a high volume hit versus a series of smaller volume niches requiring far less investment and resource.

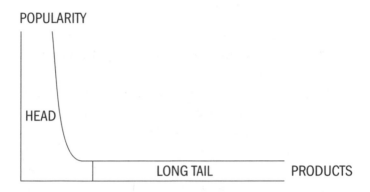

POPULARITY

HEAD

LONG TAIL   PRODUCTS

Exercise: Choose a market and identify what product and volume represents a hit. Plot this on The Long Tail diagram. Then identify a set of products that are niche, but which can be made available with minimal associated costs such as distribution and so on. Quantify each extreme to guide where the true market opportunity lies.

19 THE HISTOGRAM

- A simple classic, the histogram uses stacked oblongs to represent volume, value, percentage, or any other quantities that require comparison.
- Traditionally, the highest value is placed on the left, with the remainder ranked in descending order to the right.
- The left hand vertical axis should be given a clear and accurate scale.
- If all the data is a snapshot of one moment in time, then the horizontal axis can be left unlabelled.
- Histograms can also be used to show data over time, with each block denoting a time period such as a day, week, month or year.
- If you are drawing a time-based histogram, then the units of time need to be clearly labelled on the horizontal axis, as in Jan, Feb, Mar, etc.

AMOUNT

VOLUME OR VALUE IN RANK ORDER

Exercise: Choose a data set that currently only exists in numerical format. Decide whether you want a snapshot of a moment in time, or a view over time. Convert the numbers into proportional blocks to generate the histogram. The visual representation of the data may well reveal more than just staring at a set of numbers.

- We finish this part with a fun diagram that has infuriated people for years.
- In the Gottschaldt Figurine, or nine-dot game, there are three rows of three dots, forming what looks like a box or square.
- The precise origin of the game is the source of some debate, but management thinker John Adair claims to have introduced the idea himself in 1969.
- The challenge is to join all the dots without taking your pen off the paper, using no more than four straight lines.

- There are various ways to solve it, and two possible solutions are on the next page – don't look yet if you can resist it.
- The point is that, if you think of the dots as a box, you can't solve it.
- That is why the game is the origin of the phrase *thinking outside the box.*
- However, contrary to what this piece of jargon suggests, most studies show that problems are more likely to be solved when subject to quite tight constraints, so in reality it pays to think *inside* the box.

Exercise: *Before looking at the next page, draw nine dots on a blank page as it appears in the diagram. Now try to join all the dots using no more than four lines, and without taking the pen off the paper.*

GOTTSCHALDT FIGURINE SOLUTIONS

Solution Nº 1

Solution N° 2

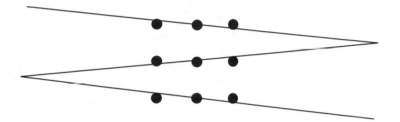

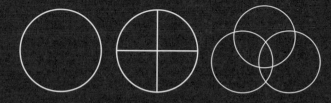

PART THREE

CIRCLES AND PIES

A WORD ON CIRCLES AND PIES

Stone circles. Crop circles. The circle of life. Hitting the bull's-eye.

Pies, fried eggs, onions, targets. Everyone loves a circle.

Circles offer the ability to handle huge amounts of data.

Quantities as a proportion of a greater whole are often easier to grasp as segments.

They are superb for highlighting subject matter and isolating elements.

Circles are complete in their own right, and so are ideal for concepts that need to be whole but do not need to specify direction.

Empty circles can be used to show overlap areas.

Circle size can represent volume or importance, and offer the chance to show satellite relationships.

It's an endless cycle of possibility.

21 THE TARGET, FRIED EGG OR ONION

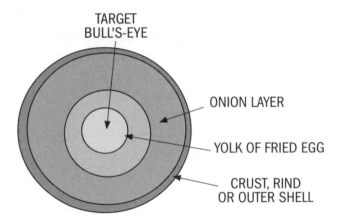

TARGET BULL'S-EYE

ONION LAYER

YOLK OF FRIED EGG

CRUST, RIND OR OUTER SHELL

- Simply drawing one circle inside another opens up a world of possibilities.
- The centre can be viewed as the yolk of an egg, the bull's-eye in a target, the core of an apple, or even the centre of the earth.
- This can be taken to be the focal point of an issue, the essence, the inner workings, or the point of origin of something.

- In one version of the diagram, the outer area is seen as the circle of concern (all the stuff people are concerned about), whereas they should be concentrating on the circle of influence (the bit in the middle they can actually have a bearing on).
- The outer layer can also represent encasement, a broader world, or simply a larger pool of something – customers or the prospective size of an opportunity.
- Additional layers can then demonstrate gradation, as in the layers of an onion, or an outer shell such as the rind of a fruit.
- The width of each layer can be adjusted to represent the volume of the task, audience or issue in question.

Exercise: *Choose a subject where quantities need to be displayed. Draw a circle to represent the complete issue or number. Place a small circle at the core. Add layers as appropriate, taking time to consider their proportion in relation to each other. Try envisaging the diagram as a fruit, vegetable, target, or other object that might inspire a useful title or analogy to articulate the issue.*

22 THE PIE CHART

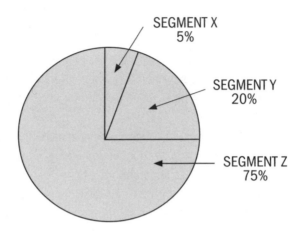

- The Pie Chart is a classic way to represent data or segments of a larger whole.
- Usually each segment is proportional to its percentage – in this case 75%, 20% and 5%.
- If there are multiple segments, then the percentage quantity of each may need to be labelled numerically for clarity.
- Colouring each segment differently helps to give definition for a snapshot at a glance.
- If there are more than six segments the diagram will probably be too confusing and so another approach may be needed – probably a histogram.

Exercise: Choose an issue where its quantity can be expressed in percentages. Try to have no more than six component parts. Convert the percentages into the correct volumes and show them as segments of the pie. Colour code and add descriptive numbers if helpful. Use the diagram to spark a new thought about how to view the issue.

23 THE VENN DIAGRAM

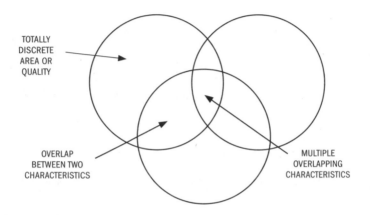

TOTALLY
DISCRETE
AREA OR
QUALITY

OVERLAP
BETWEEN TWO
CHARACTERISTICS

MULTIPLE
OVERLAPPING
CHARACTERISTICS

- Venn Diagrams were studied in detail by John Venn in 1880, although he called them Euler diagrams after Leonhard Euler who looked at them a century before.
- This is a highly flexible system of interlocking circles that are useful for identifying the contrast between overlapping qualities or areas of uniqueness.
- The minimum number of circles is two, and the maximum for most uses is three. (Highly advanced set theorists have gone as far as 16 intersections, but this is too complex for business purposes.)

- Once the circles are interlocked, totally discrete areas are revealed (in which there is no overlap). These can then be compared with the qualities of the overlap areas.
- Where three circles are used, the central area will show multiple overlapping characteristics.
- The volume of areas revealed should ideally be kept approximately proportional to their percentage of overlap so that the extent of the common ground is visually representative.

Exercise: Choose two subjects with related but not identical properties. Arrange two circles to overlap in a proportion that accurately represents their degree of common ground. Also look at the discrete areas where there is no overlap. Make decisions based on the benefits of either common ground or uniqueness.

24 THE CENTRAL IDEA
SATELLITE SYSTEM

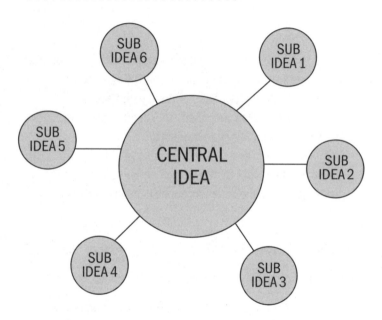

- The Central Idea Satellite System uses circles as representations of ideas or concepts, and links them together in a layout reminiscent of satellites orbiting around a central planet.
- The central idea or thought usually sits in the centre, and is represented by the largest circle on the diagram to denote its importance.
- Smaller satellites are then spun around it, normally

a minimum of three and a suggested maximum of six.

- Thematically these satellite ideas should be related to the central thought.
- They could be variations on the theme, or different media through which it can be expressed, or different audiences receiving the message, and so on, so long as all the orbiting thoughts are cousins in some way.

Exercise: Identify a central thought and place it in the centre of the system. Draw up a list of related sub-themes. Arrange them in smaller bubbles around the central thought. If necessary, start a new diagram to display a different family of sub-thoughts. Use the diagram to demonstrate the breadth and application of the main theme.

25 THE MOLECULAR STRUCTURE

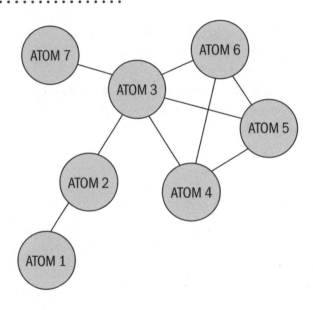

- The Molecular Structure takes its inspiration from the world of atoms and molecules.
- It is most useful for explaining the relationship between constituent parts of a more complex whole.
- It is particularly flexible inasmuch as it is not required to be uniform or symmetrical, and so can have an infinite number of constructions, with elements constantly being added or taken away.

- Each atom represents an element of the whole.
- As an example, imagine the diagram as a depiction of the components of a brand strategy, or perhaps an organization.
- The lines between each atom demonstrate some form of link. There may be only one link between one atom and another, as with atoms 1 and 2, or 3 and 7. Or there may be multiple links, as with the cluster of atoms 3, 4, 5, and 6.
- This enables the accurate depiction of individual or group links to reflect relationships or interrelationships.

Exercise: Choose a subject, perhaps an organizational structure. Represent each component as a circle. Work out how they are related to each other by drawing a line connecting the parts that are linked. Re-draw the diagram if necessary to bring clarity to how it all works.

26 THE WORK/LIFE BALANCE DIAGRAM

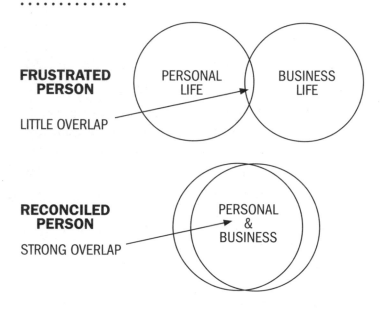

FRUSTRATED PERSON

LITTLE OVERLAP

PERSONAL LIFE

BUSINESS LIFE

RECONCILED PERSON

STRONG OVERLAP

PERSONAL & BUSINESS

- This iteration of the venn diagram is helpful in determining whether you have a sensible work/life balance.
- The two circles represent your personal and business lives – that is to say the degree to which your character is broadly the same at work and in your spare time, and whether the nature of your work bears any relation to things that interest you in your spare time.

- Those with little overlap are leading two quite separate lives, and this often leads to frustration.
- Those with strong overlap tend to be better reconciled – not having to change their character at work, and generally working on things that interest them.

Exercise: Use the two circles to depict your work and non-work character. Display the amount of overlap and try to make the degree of overlap proportional. Repeat if necessary for the nature of your work in relation to what interests you generally. If the overlap is small, work out your main frustration and see if you want to make some changes to your work or working hours.

27 THE CHANGING ROLE OF THE TEAM LEADER CIRCLE

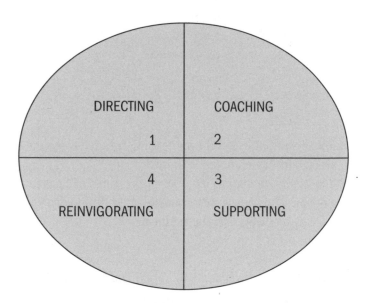

- The Changing Role of the Team Leader Circle is very helpful for working out how to deal with members of a team who may have different experience levels.
- In section one, the leader directs their subordinate, safe in the knowledge that they know what they are doing and can be left to it.
- In section two, the leader needs to coach the team member

because they have not done the task before and need to be taught how to do it.

- In section three, the person knows pretty much what they are doing but may need some back-up, so the leader needs to perform a supporting role.
- In section four, the person has done the task so many times before that they need careful motivation, so the leader needs to reinvigorate their enthusiasm.
- It is important to note that the same individual might be in a different position for each of four different tasks, even on the same day, depending on their previous experience.

Exercise: *Choose a member of your team. Write down five or six tasks that you typically need them to carry out. Work out which state of affairs applies to your role as their team leader on each job. If you are unsure, ask them how comfortable they feel in carrying out the tasks. Repeat for each member of the team, and use it as a guide to your role when next delegating work.*

28 THE CONE OR LOUD HAILER

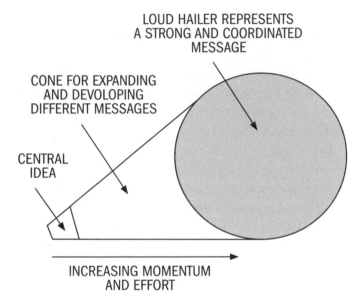

LOUD HAILER REPRESENTS
A STRONG AND COORDINATED
MESSAGE

CONE FOR EXPANDING
AND DEVOLOPING
DIFFERENT MESSAGES

CENTRAL
IDEA

INCREASING MOMENTUM
AND EFFORT

- The Cone or Loud Hailer is an interesting way to design a strategy for communication that involves multiple messages.
- The thin end or mouthpiece is a diagrammatic representation of the central idea.
- The body of the cone denotes the area in which the idea is expanded and developed into different versions of the message to suit different objectives and audiences.

- Momentum and effort should increase the more these messages are developed.
- The large circular opening on the right represents the full force of the coordinated campaign, in which all the individual messages combine to maximum effect.

Exercise: Choose a communications campaign. Place the central idea to the left of the cone. Use the body of the cone to record all the different versions of the method required for different audiences or media. Have them come together as a coordinated whole on the far right.

29 THE SO WHAT? CYCLE OF QUESTIONS

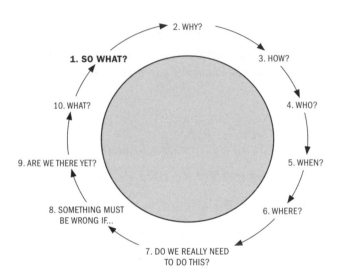

- The *So What?* Cycle of Questions is a useful ten-point process to make sure that ideas and projects actually get done.
- *So What?* is the initial screening question, effectively asking what the point of the project is. Assuming this is satisfactorily answered, then explaining why provides the rationale.
- The system then moves on to asking how, when, and where the activity will get done, and who exactly will be doing it.

- Once all these elements have been thought through in a satisfactory way, there are a number of sense-check questions to make sure that nothing has been overlooked.
- These are *Do we really need to do this?*, *Something must be wrong if...*(a sentence that requires completion), and *Are we there yet?*
- The *What?* question is left as a postscript at the end. If this hasn't been properly defined, then you may decide not to embark on the task at all.

Exercise: *Choose a project. Write down the ten questions. Answer each in sequence with a maximum of one sentence. If you cannot generate a satisfactory answer to a question, do not continue with the others. Instead consider whether to abandon or re-think the idea.*

30 THE 'FROM YOUR HEAD TO THE WORLD' CIRCLE

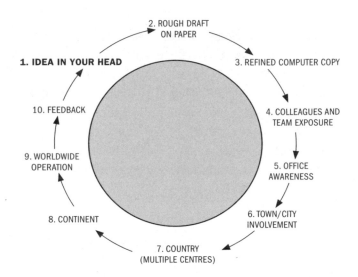

2. ROUGH DRAFT ON PAPER

1. IDEA IN YOUR HEAD

3. REFINED COMPUTER COPY

10. FEEDBACK

4. COLLEAGUES AND TEAM EXPOSURE

9. WORLDWIDE OPERATION

5. OFFICE AWARENESS

8. CONTINENT

6. TOWN/CITY INVOLVEMENT

7. COUNTRY (MULTIPLE CENTRES)

- The 'From Your Head To The World' circle is a system that helps you to work out how to get your thoughts across to others effectively.
- All ideas start in your head and the challenge is how to convey them as you intend.
- The first step is to commit a rough draft to paper, live with it for a while, and then produce a refined computer copy.

- The idea or thinking should then be test-driven on colleagues and team members before working out how to announce it in your office.
- The level of exposure thereafter depends on the scale of your operation, but could include town, city, country, continent, or even worldwide communication.
- At each level there will be different considerations about how best to communicate, and the same method will not necessarily apply in every instance.

Exercise: Select an idea that you need to reveal or share with others. Create a rough draft and then tidy it up. Test it out on some colleagues. Work out who else needs to understand, approve, or enact it. Decide on a suitable method for best communicating at each level. Put the plan together and then enact it.

PART FOUR

TIMELINES AND YEAR VIEWS

A WORD ON
TIMELINES
AND YEAR VIEWS

Time – a concept invented by man to stop everything happening at once.

Lines of time can be divided in scores of different ways.

Breaking the year into different sizes of time can be revealing.

Strategy, energy and motivation can all be seen in a new way.

And individuals and companies might even find it easier to hit their deadlines.

31 THE LIVELINE

INITIATE   COMPLETE

                                                  DEADLINE

                    LIVELINE

CONCENTRATE   IGNORE

- A deadline is a time limit for any activity.
- The biggest mistake that everybody makes when dealing with deadlines is to concentrate on the deadline rather than the bit that comes before.
- The Liveline should be 99% longer than the deadline.
- The length of a deadline, or moment of launch, will depend on the length of the Liveline. For example, a one-hour liveline might have a one-minute deadline, whereas a five year project might take one day to reveal.

- So once you have allocated the deadline, don't spend any more time concentrating on it.
- Decide the deadline, initiate the project, and then spend all your time concentrating on the Liveline that constitutes 99% of the work required.

Exercise: Choose a project. Work out the amount of time it will take. Define the duration and nature of the deadline. Now work backwards, concentrating on the Liveline. Concentrate on the length of it, and plan what needs to be done at sensible intervals long before the deadline.

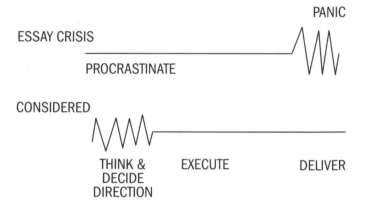

- The Personal Deadline examines the problem that most people leave things too late before they start a task.
- For most people this was a habit they acquired at college when faced with a deadline for handing in an essay or dissertation.
- Common sense suggests that a measured approach over the time available would yield a less stressed run-up and a higher quality result, but human nature dictates otherwise and many leave everything to the last minute.
- This timeline helps to focus the mind on the task ahead while there is still plenty of time.

- The considered line shows that it pays to examine as much of the material and as many of the important issues as early as possible.
- Once direction is decided, then orderly execution of the work can be embarked on, with completion being achieved smoothly.
- The idea is to avoid an Essay Crisis in which the thinking phase is left too late and hasty work is crammed in at the very end under unnecessary time pressure. The old cliché *"I work better under pressure"* is false and misleading.

Exercise: Choose a project with a known deadline, preferably no less than one week away. Work backwards from the due date to work out how much effort will be needed to complete it. Decide direction immediately, or no later than tomorrow. Initiate the execution in an orderly fashion over the remaining time.

33 THE CULTURAL DEADLINE

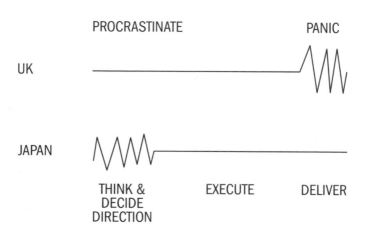

UK — PROCRASTINATE ... PANIC

JAPAN — THINK & DECIDE DIRECTION ... EXECUTE ... DELIVER

- This Cultural Deadline demonstrates that different cultures approach deadlines in different ways.
- Consider this diagram as a hypothetical time line for the launch of a product being manufactured and marketed by the Japanese and the British. The two countries are just examples.
- The Japanese line shows them grappling with their problems early, deciding direction and moving out of the thinking phase as quickly as possible, and in plenty of time to deliver.
- The UK line shows them panicking at the last moment having failed to tackle the hard stuff early.
- The second approach is more likely to produce an excellent

product on time because it adheres to the philosophy of *"Do the worst first."*

- This is because if something unexpected crops up, there is still time to deal with it without affecting the deadline.
- It also allows slippage time in which to make mistakes, pursue lines of inquiry that do not ultimately prove fruitful, change your mind, or simply have a better idea.

Exercise: *Choose a significant project. Examine the cultural tendencies in your company. Consider the approaches of all the parties involved. Anticipate those who are likely to be inclined to procrastinate. Devise a plan that deals with the difficult decisions as early in the timeline as possible.*

34 THE YEAR TO A VIEW

ACTIVITY
PRIORITY

- The Year to a View is a classic calendar diagram.
- It represents the Gregorian calendar that was officially introduced by Pope Gregory XIII in 1582.
- As such, it is divided into twelve months in an attempt to reflect the equinoxes, which is perfectly fine but doesn't necessarily mean it is a helpful timeline for businesses.
- For better or worse, all the businesses in the world use a Year to a View to represent their financial performance (the financial year), and most divide the year into four quarters, or periods of three months.

- While these dictate the content of the horizontal axis, all sorts of different variables can be used on the vertical.
- In this instance, the vertical criterion is priority of project importance, and they have been spread over the four quarters in sequence.
- The diagram is probably the universally recognized way of seeing a year's activity at a glance.

Exercise: Choose a year-long time period. Choose a subject for the vertical axis. Place the subject matter in sequence throughout the year. Use the result as a planning tool to anticipate timings and resource needs.

YEAR VIEW

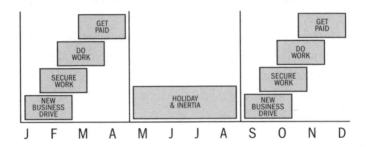

- The Tertials v. Quarters Year View provides an alternative way of carving up the year.
- In many businesses, quarters are unsatisfactory units of time because they are slightly too short to provide a helpful view of what is happening.
- A tertial is a four-month view designed to allow a business to initiate a new business drive in the first month, secure some work in the second, do the work in the third, and get paid in the fourth, thereby concluding a proper cycle of work that can be planned effectively or analyzed afterwards.

- Mapping the year in this way often reveals different findings than when using conventional quarters.
- For example, the summer tertial from May to August will almost certainly be less productive than the other two. This phasing may be different in particularly seasonal businesses.

Exercise: *Take your current year view, which is almost certainly divided into quarters. Recast the shape using tertials instead. If your business has a particular seasonal pattern move the start dates of the tertials to the months that make the most sense. Consider whether it might be more helpful to plan the year like this in future.*

36 THE LESS-THAN-TWELVE-MONTH YEAR

Productive: 6 months (above average)
Underproductive: 6 months (below average)
Decision Windows (D):   M/M/S
Crisis bombs (*):   J/A/A

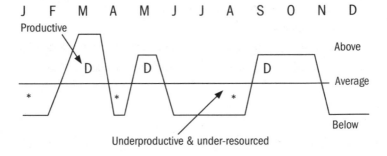

Underproductive & under-resourced

- The Less-Than-Twelve-Month Year is a diagram that makes a philosophical point about activity, or the lack of it at certain times, in companies.
- On the surface, businesses are active for twelve months a year, but in truth there are plenty of periods when they are not very productive, and this diagram helps to work out when those times are likely to be.
- All businesses have different rhythms, but in this example the most productive (above average periods) are in March, May and September.

- In these 'decision windows', every important decision maker is present, things get decided, and they get done.
- From time to time, 'crisis bombs' go off – unexpected developments that are unhelpful (in this example, this happens in January, April and August). They take up a lot of time and energy and deflect the company from its normal work, making its performance below average.
- By looking at the pattern of previous years, most of these events can be predicted and allowed for. Often this tallies with simple holiday patterns, but not always.
- Viewing the year in this way usually shows that the 'twelve month year' is almost always 'shorter' than you think.

Exercise: *Look at the year ahead. Predict the likely highly productive periods, and the unproductive ones. If necessary, predict when the decision windows and crisis bombs will occur. Now add up the truly productive months and consider reviewing any forecasts and resource planning you have undertaken.*

37 THE STRATEGY V. TACTICS YEAR VIEW

OVERARCHING THOUGHT (THE STRATEGY)

EXAMPLES AND PROOF (TACTICS)

TACTIC 1	TACTIC 2	TACTIC 3	TACTIC 4

J F M A M J J A S O N D

- One of the trickiest things businesses struggle with is the difference between strategy and tactics, and how to plan their shape.
- The Strategy v. Tactics Year View helps to clarify matters.
- The strategy is the overarching thought, here shown as a top block or lintel. This is the consistent theme and direction that never varies, and against which all other activities can be judged and measured.

- The tactics are specific examples or proof of the strategy, and their deployment must have a clear beginning and end.
- The year view helps clearly distinguish the two elements, and enables you to map out precisely when the tactical initiatives should occur.

Exercise: *Look at the year ahead. Decide on the overall strategy and place it as a constant overarching theme. Choose an appropriate number of tactics and place them in the right time segment. Look at the total picture and decide if it is suitably balanced. Use the year view to explain the plan to colleagues.*

38 THE ENERGY LINE

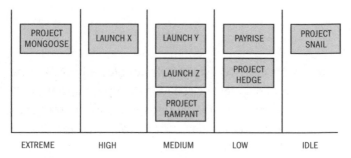

PROJECT MONGOOSE	LAUNCH X	LAUNCH Y	PAYRISE	PROJECT SNAIL
		LAUNCH Z	PROJECT HEDGE	
		PROJECT RAMPANT		
EXTREME	HIGH	MEDIUM	LOW	IDLE

ENERGY LEVEL

- The Energy Line was suggested in 2010 by Scott Belsky in his book *Making Ideas Happen*.
- Most companies and their staff have far too many projects on the go at once, and as such their most precious commodity is energy because they only have a finite amount of it and can't do everything at the same time.
- The idea is to place your projects along an Energy Line according to how much energy they should receive, as in the diagram.
- It is important to note that this categorization is not based on how much time you are spending on a project – energy now is not the same as time in total over a project lifespan.

- Classifying your work this way prompts questions about the degree to which you are focusing on the right things.

Exercise: Draw up a list of all your projects. Place each one in one of the categories, from extreme to Idle. Remember to concentrate on energy level, not time spent. Move them around until the priority is right. Repeat the process as often as is necessary depending on the number and average duration of your projects.

39 THE MOTIVATIONAL DIP

ENERGY

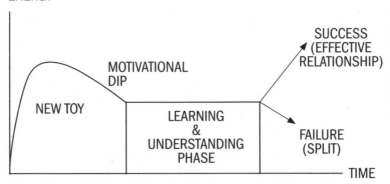

- The Motivational Dip is another way of looking at energy and application of resource. It can be used to analyze just one project or an entire relationship.
- It looks at enthusiasm over time, and can be used to predict the moments when things are likely to lose momentum and slip.
- The vertical axis represents amount of energy devoted to a task or relationship.
- The horizontal time axis maps the stages that motivation levels will probably go through.
- Things typically start well with a 'new toy' mentality – the honeymoon phase.

- A Motivational Dip is usually experienced before a more settled learning and understanding phase kicks in.
- After this, the project either moves on to success and completion, or fizzles out in failure.
- The relationship version of this final phase will determine whether two parties working together, such as a client and their agency, will establish an effective relationship or split up.

Exercise: Choose a project or relationship that is just about to start. Plot the likely phases and work out when the Motivational Dip is likely to occur. Put measures in place to counteract it. You can also apply the method retrospectively to see when things went wrong and learn how to improve matters in the future.

40 THE MOTIVATIONAL
CLOTHES LINE

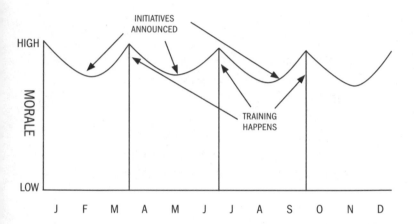

- The Motivational Clothes Line enables managers and especially Human Resources managers to plan and pace initiatives to optimum effect throughout the year.
- The vertical axis represents staff morale, and naturally we want this to be as high as possible as often as possible.
- The peaks, or tops of the clothes line poles, represent the moments of highest morale, and these coincide with training initiatives or other efforts that the company makes to help staff.

- Not surprisingly, this declines over time after the event.
- The knack for managers is to predict the point at which this should fall no lower lest it become detrimental. This is precisely when the next initiative should be announced, thus sending morale upward again in anticipation of the event.
- By planning the year in this way, managers can ensure that morale never falls below a certain level, and can avoid criticism that the company is doing nothing for their staff, since at any given moment something has just happened, or is going to soon.

Exercise: Plot the minimum and maximum realistic morale levels for the year. Choose a suitable number of initiatives that will improve matters. Space them appropriately throughout the year. Use the Motivational Clothes Line to strike the right balance between the number of events and their effect on morale levels.

PART FIVE

FLOWS AND CONCEPTS

A WORD ON FLOWS AND CONCEPTS

Some ideas need flow. They may need to meander.

Work needs to flow in organizations, and people need to know how it's going to work.

Flows certainly need to demonstrate movement.

They can be temporal. Or directional. Or suggestive of a process of some kind.

They can also represent processes of the mind – concepts.

Rivers, dams, funnels, hoppers, and buckets. If it's to do with water it might help an idea along.

41 THE ORGANIZATION CHART: HOW TO DO IT

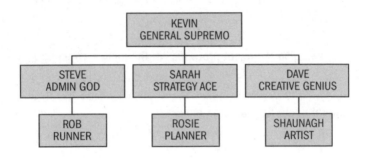

- An organization chart needs to be crystal clear.
- Its purpose is to explain to the people represented in it how they are supposed to interact with their colleagues. It should also be capable of explaining to a potential client how a company is organized.
- A clear chart should allow anyone looking at it to work out the basic hierarchy based on who is the boss, who is the next subordinate down, and so on. These boxes should be linked with clear vertical lines.

- Descriptions of what role the individuals perform can be added if it helps, or the entire process can be carried out just for department functions rather than people and roles.
- Dotted lines do not work because they cause confusion about who reports to whom.
- Cross-reports and multiple bosses should also be avoided.

Exercise: *Either choose an existing organization chart or start from scratch. Work out who reports to whom in a simple hierarchy. Map it out with vertical lines. Add job descriptions if necessary. Avoid cross-reports, dotted lines and multiple bosses. Use the chart to clarify roles, or to identify relationships that are simply too complex.*

42 THE ORGANIZATION CHART: HOW NOT TO DO IT

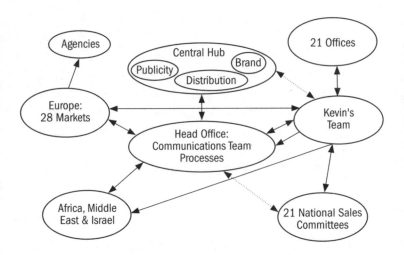

- This is a chart I was once given to 'explain' how an advertising agency worked with an international client. If anybody can understand how it works, do please get in touch.
- Organization charts are a major culprit when it comes to the golden rule of diagrams – that their primary purpose is to clarify and inform.
- This diagram has a number of faults.
- First, it contains 11 circles, which is too much.

- Second, it contains 12 arrows, which is also too much.
- Third, it contains circles within a circle, for no apparent reason.
- Fourth, it contains dotted lines, which always cause confusion.
- Fifth, there has been no attempt to relate the scale of the circles to the size of the individual or division.

Exercise: *Select a complex set of interrelationships, or find a confusing organization chart. Strip out as many components as possible. Analyze every arrow to work out what it is trying to communicate. If there is simply too much information on the chart, break it down into two or three clearer ones.*

43 THE THREE BUCKETS

BRILLIANT BASICS   **COMPELLING DIFFERENCE**   **CHANGING THE GAME**

- The Three Buckets exercise was introduced by Adam Morgan in his book *The Pirate Inside* in 2004.
- It is an extremely helpful way to categorize projects and work out how effective they are likely to be.
- Each project must be placed in one of the three buckets.
- On the left is Brilliant Basics. These represent "excellence as standard". You or your company should be doing these well as a matter of course, just like your competitors.
- In the middle is "compelling difference". These should be "significantly better than normal". These are demonstrably better than your competitors, but not genuinely remarkable.

- On the right is Changing The Game. These are "truly extraordinary". They are utterly unique in the market, and genuinely remarkable.
- This exercise will reveal whether a sufficient proportion of the projects are going to make a genuine difference.

Exercise: *Take a list of all existing projects. Scrutinize them by the three sets of criteria and place them in the relevant bucket. Look at the quantity in each. Review whether the balance is right. Use the findings to cancel unnecessary projects or search for more enterprising ones.*

44 THE FUNNEL, HOPPER OR LEAKY BUCKET

BUSINESS IN

PROSPECTS

NEW CUSTOMERS

OLD CUSTOMERS

EX-CUSTOMERS

BUSINESS OUT

- This diagram can be viewed as a narrowing funnel, a tapering grain hopper, or a plain old bucket.
- In most instances the wider top represents a larger volume or number.
- In this example, it is being used to look at the process of acquiring new customers.
- There are a large number of prospects who are not yet customers, and eventually a proportion become so.

- Over time new customers become old ones, and this increases the chances of them experiencing a problem with the product or service.
- If this dissatisfaction is not dealt with effectively, then they will leave and so become ex-customers.
- This sequence of "business in" to "business out" allows a company to analyze how many prospects are required to feed the business properly, and how customer satisfaction is working.
- If the volume of business leaving is too high in relation to that coming in, then it is a leaky bucket that needs urgent attention.

Exercise: Use the hopper to create a gradation from prospects to ex-customers. Populate each layer with numbers. Use the progression to work out whether the business is losing too many customers in relation to the new ones coming in. Put measures in place to rectify the discrepancy.

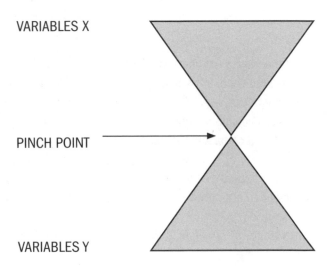

VARIABLES X

PINCH POINT

VARIABLES Y

- The Hour Glass is a highly flexible device that can be used conceptually or to demonstrate flow.
- In a conceptual context, it is often used to describe an entity that has plenty at the top and bottom, but very little in the middle.
- For example, that might be an organization that has plenty of senior management and lots of junior executives, but far fewer middle managers.
- This view can identify bottlenecks in workflow and approval procedures – as such, an hour glass business is most likely imbalanced and in need of attention.

- In a flow context, movement of materials or concepts can be viewed as starting broadly in a fair quantity at the top, whittling to a pinch point, and then expanding back outward at the base.
- An example might be considering 20 ideas, eliminating all but one of them, and then using that as a focus for everything that follows.

Exercise: Use the Hour Glass to review a large quantity of options. Whittle to the winning idea. Then expand outward to look at all its possible manifestations. Consider adding a timeline to define when all the decisions will be made, and using it as a template to guide the next project.

46 THE BOW TIE

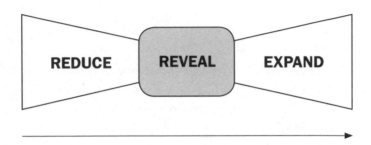

REDUCE **REVEAL** **EXPAND**

LINE OF ARGUMENT

- The Bow Tie is a horizontal cousin of the Hour Glass.
- It is a really simple depiction of how to tell an effective strategic story.
- The line of argument flows from left to right.
- Starting broadly on the left, many wide options and possibilities are considered and discussed.
- After investigation and analysis, these are gradually ruled out and reduced down.

- When the reduction of options is complete, the central idea, thought or theme is revealed.
- After pausing for a moment on the quality of what has been revealed, the idea is expanded out again to explain all its possible applications.
- This is the ideal way to tell a strategic story.

Exercise: Choose a strategy or rationale that requires explaining in a presentation. Use The Bow Tie as a template. Start broad, explain how options were reduced down, reveal the central theme, and then expand on how it can be applied in many contexts.

47 THE DECISION TREE

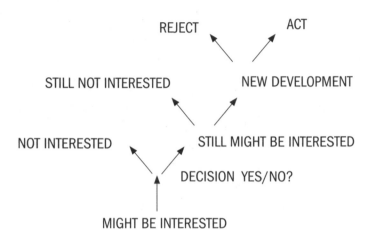

- The Decision Tree is a form of flow diagram that helps to map out complicated decision-making processes, or the possible directions a conversation or interaction might take.
- Each branch of a tree represents a decisive moment. This can be as clear cut as *yes/no*, or as mild as *not interested/ might be*.
- The tree is particularly useful in mapping long and drawn-out sales decision processes such as buying a car, which might have a three-year gestation period.

- It can also be used to map options on questionnaires, the options in call centre conversations, or those on a technological interface such as a mobile device.
- More artistic representations can be generated using images of real trees, river tributaries, pathways, arteries, and so on.

Exercise: *Choose a sales process that involves many small decisions – preferably a minimum of six steps. Plot the customer frame of mind from not interested all the way to a definite sale. Identify the defining decision moments and work out how to influence them in your favour.*

48 THE RIVERS AND DAMS CONCEPT

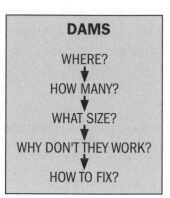

RIVERS	DAMS
WHERE?	WHERE?
↓	↓
HOW MANY?	HOW MANY?
↓	↓
WHAT SIZE?	WHAT SIZE?
↓	↓
WHY DO THEY WORK?	WHY DON'T THEY WORK?
↓	↓
WHERE ELSE TO USE?	HOW TO FIX?

- The Rivers and Dams Concept looks at the flow of work in a company, and how well it functions.
- Rivers are things that work well. They run smoothly.
- Dams are blockages. They don't work well and they hold things up.
- In both cases, the first three questions are the same: where are they, how many are there, and what size are they?

- Since rivers are good, we then want to know why they work so well, and decide where else in the company we could use them.
- Since dams are bad, we need to know why they don't work, and work out how to fix them.
- If there is a large quantity of either to be dealt with, then the size question in each case enables a level of priority to be set on what to deal with first.

Exercise: Choose a department, the whole company, or a particular process that needs examination. Identify and categorize the rivers and dams. Run through the sequence of questions in each case. Now draw up a plan to increase the good things and fix the bad ones.

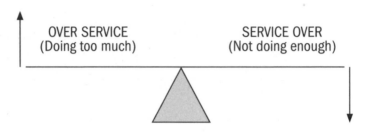

OVER SERVICE
(Doing too much)

SERVICE OVER
(Not doing enough)

- The Service Fulcrum examines the delicate balancing act between under- and over-delivery in service industries.
- The triangular fulcrum sits in the middle, and the horizontal line represents a well-balanced state of affairs – the correct amount of work being delivered to reflect the needs of the customer and the price being paid.
- If the service company does too much, they will be over servicing and thus eroding their margin – sometimes to the point of only breaking even, or even making a loss.
- If the service company does not do enough, it will be under-servicing and therefore failing to meet the needs of the customer. If this is the case, the service may well be 'over' because the customer might move the business.

- The diagram can be viewed alongside data (such as man hours, pricing and margin) to dramatize in what way the service level is imbalanced.

Exercise: Choose a service relationship. Gather information about how it works, such as time spent, margin and profitability. See whether the company is over- or under-servicing. Take appropriate action.

50 THE DEPERSONALIZING
PROBLEMS CONCEPT

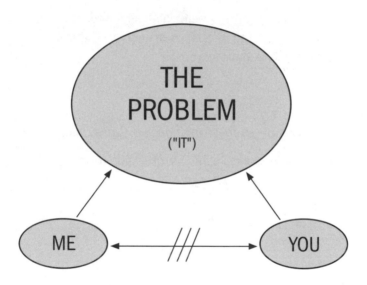

- The Depersonalizing Problems concept helps to calm things down when everything has become too personal for comfort.
- Often in business, frustration with an aspect of work is centred on an individual rather than the issue. When this happens, language can become too personal.

- The horizontal line between 'me' and 'you' running across the bottom represents two people getting at each other, and the hashed vertical lines struck through it dramatize that language such as 'I', 'me', and 'you' don't work and should be avoided.
- Instead, the problem should be viewed as a large balloon, and should be described as 'it'.
- The plural 'we' should replace 'I', 'me', and 'you' when discussing the issue.
- Example phraseology might be: *"This is a serious problem isn't it? There are various different ways that we can use to solve it."*

Exercise: *Find an issue that has become too personal. Remove personal language from the discussion. Start looking at the problem as 'it'. Now propose solutions with the collective 'we'. Suggest the method to any colleagues who are getting at each other.*

APPENDIX
Diagram Sources and Further Reading

All diagrams are originated by the author unless otherwise stated.

3. The Cone of Learning: Edgar Dale 1969
18. The Long Tail: *The Long Tail*, Chris Anderson (Random House, 2006)
20. The Gottschaldt Figurine: *Flicking Your Creative Switch*, Wayne Lotherington (John Wiley, 2003); *The Art Of Creative Thinking*, John Adair (Kogan Page, 1990)
38. The Energy Line: *Making Ideas Happen*, Scott Belsky (Portfolio, 2010)
43. The Three Buckets: *The Pirate Inside*, Adam Morgan (John Wiley, 2004)

More detail and examples can be found in the following books:

Run Your Own Business, Kevin Duncan (Hodder & Stoughton, 2010)
Small Business Survival, Kevin Duncan (Hodder & Stoughton, 2010)
So What?, Kevin Duncan (Capstone, 2008)
Tick Achieve, Kevin Duncan (Capstone, 2008)

Other helpful organizational books:

Execution, Bossidy & Sharan (Crown Business, 2002)
Getting Things Done, David Allen (Piatkus, 2001)
Simply Brilliant, Fergus O'Connell (Pearson, 2001)

ABOUT THE AUTHOR

Kevin Duncan is a business adviser, marketing expert, motivational speaker and author. After 20 years in advertising, he has spent the last 15 as an independent troubleshooter, advising companies on how to change their businesses for the better, via change management programmes, non-exec work or better pitching.

Contact the author for advice and training:
kevinduncanexpertadvice@gmail.com
expertadviceonline.com
thediagramsbook.com

Also by the author:
The Ideas Book
Business Greatest Hits
Catch-11
Marketing Greatest Hits
Marketing Greatest Hits Volume 2
Revolution
Run Your Own Business
Small Business Survival
So What?
Start
The Dictionary of Business Bullshit
Tick Achieve
What You Need To Know About Starting A Business

BEYOND
THE WRITTEN WORD

Authors who speak to you face to face.

Discover LID Speakers, a service that enables businesses to have direct and interactive contact with the best ideas brought to their own sector by the most outstanding creators of business thinking.

- **A network specialising in business speakers, making it easy to find the most suitable candidates.**

- **A website with full details and videos, so you know exactly who you're hiring.**

- **A forum packed with ideas and suggestions about the most interesting and cutting-edge issues.**

- **A place where you can make direct contact with the best in international speakers.**

- **The only speakers' bureau backed up by the expertise of an established business book publisher.**